FRANCIS FRITH'S
TOWN & CITY
MEMORIES

LEAMINGTON SPA

GRAHAM SUTHERLAND is a retired police inspector, and has lived and worked for many years in the Leamington Spa area. He is Beadle and Town Crier of Warwick and an author and lecturer on local, historical and criminological and social subjects. A founder member of the Leamington Archaeology Group and the Leamington Guild of Guides, he is a member of the Warwickshire Local History and Warwickshire Constabulary History Societies; and a Heart of England Registered Blue Badge Tour Guide.

FRANCIS FRITH'S

TOWN & CITY

MEMORIES

LEAMINGTON SPA

GRAHAM SUTHERLAND

FRANCIS FRITH'S
TOWN&CITY
MEMORIES

First published as Leamington Spa, A Photographic History of your Town
in 2001 by Black Horse Books, an imprint of The Francis Frith Collection
Revised edition published in the United Kingdom in 2006 by
The Francis Frith Collection as Leamington Spa, Town and City Memories
Limited Hardback Edition ISBN 1-84589-148-1
Paperback Edition ISBN 1-84589-149-X

British Library Cataloguing in Publication Data

Leamington Spa
Town and City Memories
Graham Sutherland

The Francis Frith Collection®
Frith's Barn, Teffont,
Salisbury, Wiltshire SP3 5QP
Tel: +44 (0) 1722 716 376
Email: info@francisfrith.co.uk
www.francisfrith.com

Aerial photographs reproduced under licence from Simmons Aerofilms Limited
Historical Ordnance Survey maps reproduced under licence from Homecheck.co.uk

Printed and bound in England

Front Cover: LEAMINGTON SPA, Royal Pump Room & Parish Church 1922 72442t
The colour-tinting in this image is for illustrative purposes only,
and is not intended to be historically accurate

FRANCIS FRITH'S

TOWN & CITY

MEMORIES

CONTENTS

FRANCIS FRITH, Victorian founder of the world-famous photographic archive, was a devout Quaker and a highly successful Victorian businessman. By 1860 he was already a multi-millionaire, having established and sold a wholesale grocery business in Liverpool. He had also made a series of pioneering photographic journeys to the Nile region. The images he returned with were the talk of London. An eminent modern historian has likened their impact on the population of the time to that on our own generation of the first photographs taken on the surface of the moon.

Frith had a passion for landscape, and was as equally inspired by the countryside of Britain as he was by the desert regions of the Nile. He resolved to set out on a new career and to use his skills with a camera. He established a business in Reigate as a specialist publisher of topographical photographs.

Frith lived in an era of immense and sometimes violent change. For the poor in the early part of Victoria's reign work was a drudge and the hours long, and ordinary people had precious little free time. Most had not travelled far beyond the boundaries of their own town or village. Mass tourism was in its infancy during the 1860s, but during the next decade the railway network and the establishment of Bank Holidays and half-Saturdays gradually made it possible for the working man and his family to enjoy holidays and to see a little more of the world. With characteristic business acumen, Francis Frith foresaw that these new tourists would enjoy having souvenirs to commemorate their days out. He began selling photo-souvenirs of seaside resorts and beauty spots, which the Victorian public pasted into treasured family albums.

Frith's aim was to photograph every town and village in Britain. For the next thirty years he travelled the country by train and by pony and trap, producing fine photographs of seaside resorts and beauty spots that were keenly bought by millions of Victorians.

THE RISE OF FRITH & CO

Each photograph was taken with tourism in mind, the small team of Frith photographers concentrating on busy shopping streets, beaches, seafronts, picturesque lanes and villages. They also photographed buildings: the Victorian and Edwardian eras were times of huge building activity, and town halls, libraries, post offices, schools and technical colleges were springing up all over the country. They were invariably celebrated by a proud Victorian public, and photo souvenirs – visual records – published by F Frith & Co were sold in their hundreds of thousands. In addition, many new commercial buildings such as hotels, inns and pubs were photographed, often because their owners specifically commissioned Frith postcards or prints of them for re-sale or for publicity purposes.

In order to gain some understanding of the scale of Frith's business one only has to look at the catalogue issued by Frith & Co in 1886: it runs to some 670 pages. By 1890 Frith had created the greatest specialist photographic publishing company in the world, with over 2,000 stockists! The picture on the right shows the Frith & Co display board on the wall of the stockist at Ingleton in the Yorkshire Dales (left of window). Beautifully constructed with a mahogany frame and gilt inserts, it displayed a dozen scenes.

POSTCARD BONANZA

The ever-popular holiday postcard we know today took many years to appear, and F Frith & Co was in the vanguard of its development. Postcards became a hugely popular means of communication and sold in their millions. Frith's company took full advantage of this boom and soon became the major publisher of photographic view postcards.

Francis Frith died in 1898 at his villa in Cannes, his great project still growing. His sons Eustace and Cyril continued their father's monumental task, expanding the number of views offered to the public and recording more and more places in Britain, as the coasts and countryside were opened up to mass travel. The archive Frith created

continued in business for another seventy years. By 1970 it contained over a third of a million pictures of 7,000 cities, towns and villages. The massive photographic record Frith has left to us stands as a living monument to a special and very remarkable man.

This book shows Leamington Spa as it was photographed by this world-famous archive at various periods in its development over the past 150 years. Every photograph was taken for a specific commercial purpose, which explains why the selection may not show every aspect of the town landscape. However, the photographs, compiled from one of the world's most celebrated archives, provide an important and absorbing record of your town.

WARWICKSHIRE COUNTY MAP

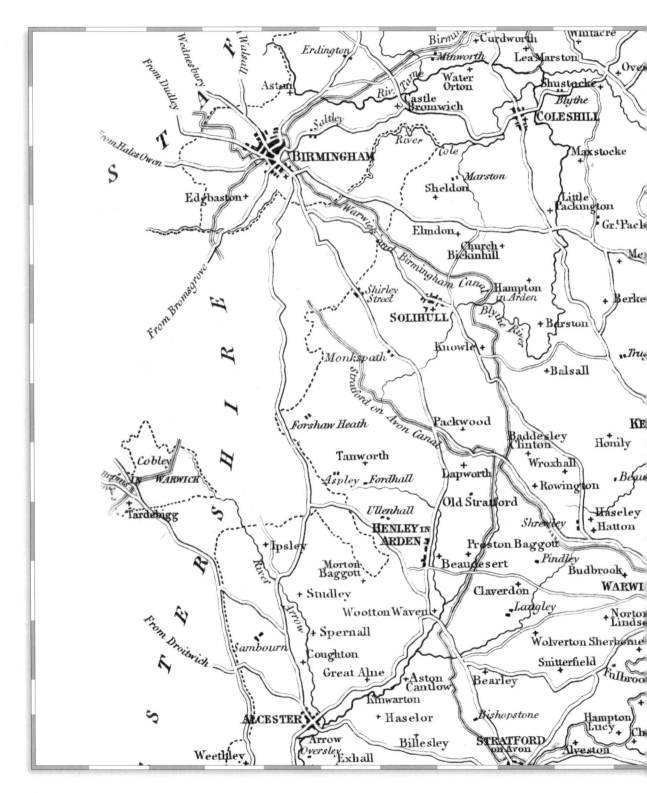

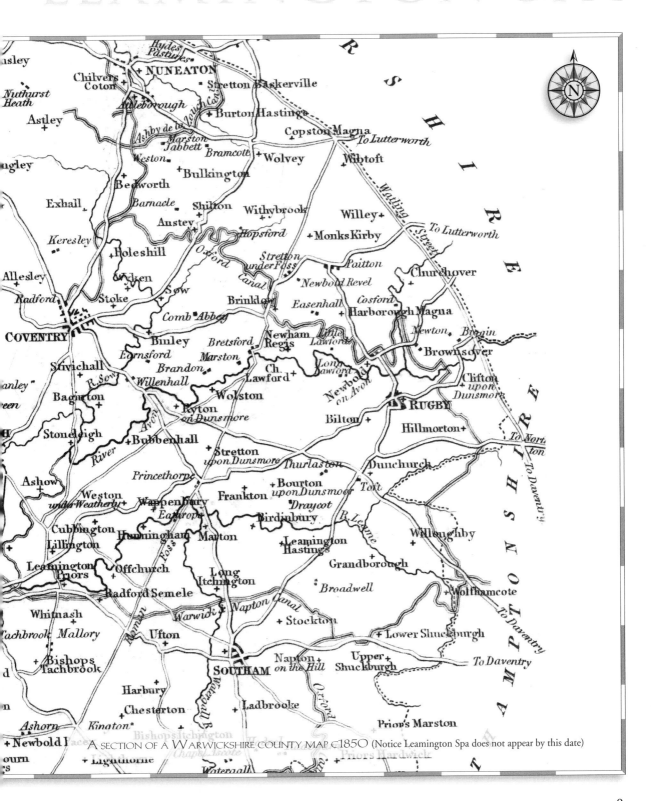

A SECTION OF A WARWICKSHIRE COUNTY MAP C1850 (Notice Leamington Spa does not appear by this date)

INTRODUCTION

THE 1881 Black's 'Guide to Warwickshire' described Leamington Spa as 'pleasantly situated on the Leam, a tributary of the Avon. From a small obscure village, it has risen in the course of 40 years to become one of the most esteemed watering places in the kingdom'.

Its prosperity stemmed from the mineral waters first discovered in 1586. Local shoemaker Benjamin Satchwell and innkeeper William Abbots established the original baths in 1794. The discovery of more springs during the next decade encouraged a considerable number of visitors. With expansion over the years, Leamington has altered considerably. The taking of the waters is now history, but their influence still remains in many parts of the town.

Leamington's first known origins are in the 7th century in the area around the river, becoming known as Leamington Priors. In 1800 its buildings consisted of one manor house, three farms and 50 labourers' cottages. This situation was due for a very rapid change. As Nathaniel Hawthorne said: 'out of this muddy ditch gushed out, as if by magic, a multitude of fine buildings of every kind.'

In spite of the efforts of Benjamin Satchwell and William Abbots, there had been little movement, due to the Napoleonic Wars and a disastrous harvest in 1799. The actual period of prosperity, whilst short, was hectic. When taking the waters became unfashionable in the 1850s, the growth of the railways made Leamington into a different type of resort. There was an influx of retired high-ranking officers, civil servants and clergymen, which led to a frantic building programme lasting for the next 30 years. But it was not without a price. As north Leamington grew, the south slipped into a cycle of depression and neglect which is still apparent today. The period following the Second World War set a new pace of housing development in and around Leamington.

THE PARADE 1932 85204 (DETAIL)

TOWN HALL 1932 85199 (DETAIL)

WARWICK STREET 1922 72445

Once an affluent street. Today the buildings on the left, once popular with dentists, are now offices. The buildings opposite are being converted into flats. Trams ran between Leamington and Warwick.

TOWN HALL 1932 85199

Once known as Union Parade, this view of the Town Hall and Parade shows how Leamington has expanded. Why is the Union Jack flying? Perhaps it has something to do with the music festival being advertised on the Town Hall. The design of the bus just passing changed little over the next 20 years. On the right is the access to Regent Grove with just a lamp post and small island to break it up. On the left, the Refuge Assurance building is now part of Barclays Bank. The Maypole Dairy has long gone. Next door is Savoury's Restaurant - the owner's name or a clever pun? The high white building was Burtons Tailors but is now a Pizza Hut which still has dancing and billiards facilities above.

INTRODUCTION

In 1875 Leamington achieved Borough status. Later, Lillington and Milverton were added amidst fierce opposition from those who did not wish to be associated with Leamington traders! The town retained responsibility for many of its services until 1947, including the police and fire departments. It had not been an easy relationship with the county. If the Chief Constables of Leamington and Warwickshire happened to be on the same street, one or both of them would attempt any manoeuvre in order to avoid having to speak. The formation of Warwick District Council in 1974 saw the end of much of Leamington's independence.

With the growth of houses and services for the wealthy, the need arose to accommodate the workers. Many servants lived in, but not so shop assistants and other employees. The first new house was built at the junction of the Parade and Regent Street, known as Cross Street before a visit by the Prince Regent. Others soon followed. As building spread, three houses in the Parade were joined and became the Bedford Hotel (now the HSBC Bank). Whilst the quality of houses for the wealthy was fine the lower classes were not so fortunate.

In 1849 Leamington suffered from a cholera outbreak in which 20 people died. The outbreak was denied in order to prevent panic and financial disaster. When it was over, there was still no better outlook for the poor. 15 years later figures record 85 people living in 16 houses; open and unfenced cesspits; 19 slaughtermen in the Warwick Street/Regent Street areas; privy buckets emptied in the street. Overcrowding continued and during the Second World War the influx of foreign troops and refugees made matters worse. Then came a post-war decline in the town accompanied by industrial expansion. By 1947 housing was inadequate and resulted in the conversion to flats of many of the older buildings and the creation of housing estates.

The London Building Act of 1774 classified

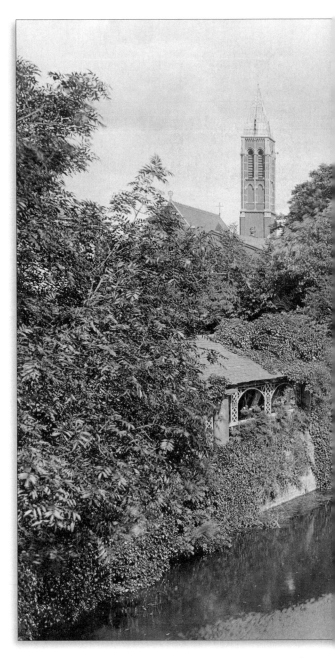

Leamington as third rate with no pretensions of grandeur. Most building designs were copied from a widely available pattern book. Balconies and iron railings were added individually. By 1850 many buildings in the Parade had become shops, at one time

This view portrays a more tranquil area of Leamington. St Peter's Pineapple Tower dominates the skyline. Half hidden in the bushes is a summerhouse for one of the properties in Dormer Place. On the right is a lifebelt which in those days could be left out in safety without fear of it being stolen or vandalised.

the highest number of retailers being bakers! There was no shortage of servants although many were only employed for 51 weeks of the year and thus unable to claim Leamington as their home and making them ineligible for parish relief. Labour had become very cheap by the early 20th century, helped by the drift of agricultural workers into domestic servants and shop assistants. Hours were long, pay was poor, absenteeism was rife. In the overcrowded houses disease was rampant. Not really the face Leamington wanted to show to the world!

THE PARADE

THE PARADE

THE PARADE'S standing as Leamington's showpiece from the earliest days has been fiercely protected over the years. This attitude is illustrated by the adverse reaction to the Golden Lion pub (which is now the Royal Bank of Scotland) being built only about 30 yards away in Regent Street. Another example was the opposition to the new tram routes running up the Parade which, it was believed, would disfigure it. One critic suggested it 'was held to be so sacred they would put it in a glass case if they could'. It was even suggested that 'working men and their wives should not walk upon it'!

CLARENDON HOTEL 1922 72450

This was one of Leamington's longer-lasting hotels. It opened in 1832 in Lansdowne Place, now Upper Parade. Recognisable by its Doric porch and pilasters, the hotel quickly built up a reputation for excellent service, and was a regular meeting place for the many who enjoyed sampling its well-kept beers served in pewter tankards. In this picture the only form of transport which can be seen is the small handcart to the right of Christ Church, possibly that of a road sweeper. The garage opposite the hotel was still operating in the 1950s. In 1983 the empty hotel was bought by Warwick Commodities broker Keith Hunt. He vanished the same year leaving behind a tangled financial web. He has not been seen since. The hotel became part of the Trust House Forte Group before its demise. It is now named Clarendon Court, and houses 24 luxury apartments.

THE PARADE

Right: REGENT HOTEL 1892 30975

Originally estimated at £15,000, the final cost of this hotel was reputedly £70-80,000. Upon completion it was thought to be the biggest hotel in Europe, with 100 bedrooms and private suites but just one bathroom! It was furnished to costly and elegant taste with stabling for 100 horses and 50 carriages. Two horse-drawn pleasure coaches ran from here until the early 1900s. Many royal and distinguished guests have visited over the years. During the Second World War it was taken over by the Camouflage Department. The imposing entrance and main staircase with stained glass background made an ideal background for wedding photographs, although some people considered this location to be too suggestive! The Regent has now become a Travelodge Hotel, with entrance in Livery Street, on the way to the new shopping mall, but still retains the old staircase complete with its stained glass. The front is now the Leamington Bar and Grill.

Below: TOWN HALL AND THE PARADE 1892 30951

Pedestrians and horse drawn vehicles are very much in evidence. The iron railings have long since gone. The Town Hall dominates this part of the Parade, and Queen Victoria's statue has yet to arrive. Christ Church can be seen at the top of the Parade.

Right: THE PARADE 1932 85201

On the right in this picture is Bedford Stores which became B & Cs. Young Charles Richard Burgis came to Leamington in 1855, setting up as a grocer. In 1874 he went into partnership with James Colbourne. Eight years later they moved into the premises on the Parade known as Athenaeum Library, home to 20,000 books, famous glass chandeliers and a ceiling dome. The Company became limited in 1897 but they were bitterly resented for the hardship their business caused smaller traders.

Initially the tram service ran eight cars in each direction daily except Sundays when there was only one. Twelve months later that had increased to 52 and 16 respectively with two extra horses to pull the cars up the Parade. The three-mile journey took about 40 minutes. 1905 saw the demise of the horse-drawn service and the birth of the electric tram whose dark green and cream cars carried up to 48 passengers. It had all finished by 1930. One morning an overhead cable became detached and it was pulled to one side by a policeman. Nobody could understand why he had not been electrocuted. The central pillars holding the cables became street lights.

The 50-bedroom Bedford Hotel opened in 1811 and was nearly always full. 128 gentlemen attended its inaugural dinner. Originally known as Williams' Hotel, it hosted the exclusive Oyster Club with very restricted membership. Gentlemen of Fortune were not admitted. Another attraction was port served in pint-sized decanters. Shropshire squire Jack Mytton earned immortal fame when he jumped his horse off the first floor balcony into the Parade. Both survived. The hotel was subsequently acquired by the Leamington Priors and Warwickshire Banking Company and is now the HSBC Bank.

The Parade has been the focal point in Leamington for many events. One was the mile-long procession to mark the end of the Crimean War in 1856. Each child was given a straw hat or bonnet. The procession ended with food and fireworks in Jephson Gardens.

It has become the major shopping area for Leamington, crossed by Warwick and Regent Streets. One of the longer-standing shops was

THE PARADE

Burgis and Colbourne, fondly known as B & Cs, currently House of Fraser. At its height, B & Cs was a department store supplying most items. Its restaurant was a popular stop for morning coffee for shoppers and staff alike.

In 1818 John Williams, proprietor of the Bedford Hotel, began building a bigger one, soon to be called Regent Hotel after the Prince Regent. Built by C S Smith of Warwick, it opened in 1819 with an inaugural dinner of venison and turtle. The original entrance was at the side and the Parade portico was added 30 years later.

TOWN HALL C1960 L25027

On the other side of the Parade the emphasis is on shops, and has been for many years. Sunblinds were used regularly with their height restricted by law. A policeman had to be able to walk underneath them without getting his helmet knocked off. There was once an extremely tall policeman in Leamington and an exception had to be made in his case. Many of these businesses have now gone, including P H Woodward. On the right is the obelisk erected in 1880 to Henry Bright who had fresh water supplied to the town. Previously it had come from the river - not a nice thought! Ironically, the water supply at the memorial's base has been sealed off.

THE PARADE

TOWN HALL C1955 L25047C

Albert Toft's statue of Queen Victoria was erected in 1902. She had visited Leamington both as a Princess and Queen. The royal train once stopped just to allow her to take tea on Leamington railway station. During the night of 14 November 1940 (the night of the huge raid on Coventry), a nearby bomb blast moved her statue on the plinth by about an inch. She has not yet been put back. No doubt she would not be amused by the arguments concerning her renovation. In this view, pedestrian facilities now cross the Parade which is much busier, but still has ample parking space. Motor vehicle design is much different from today. Christ Church still dominates the upper town, but its days are numbered. The Jacobs Biscuits delivery van could be en route to several shops on the Parade. The 'wonderfully absurd' town hall dominates this area. In front a pedestrian crossing spans the entrance to Regent Grove and Hamilton Terrace.

Left: THE PARADE 1932 85202

Sketchleys Cleaners have now gone. The hairdressers next door remind us of the times when some shops had other business premises above them. Pearl Assurance is no longer based here. Women are wearing fur stoles either for the sake of fashion or simply because it is cold — although it is warm enough for at least one car to have its roof down. Madame Wright specialised in ladies fashions and millinery.

Although businesses have come and gone the Parade has changed little over the years. Further down from the Regent is the Town Hall, designed by John Cundall and costing a mere £20,000. Originally located in High Street, it was ready for rebuilding in the 1880s. The current site was chosen in preference to the Pump Room Gardens although its building meant the demolition of Denby Villa. During the construction, 11 brothers called Smith worked on the site.

Having a mixture of red brick and brown stone formed into a Tudor Baroque front, it was considered by some to be quite out of keeping with the rest of Leamington. The building has been described as 'wonderfully absurd'. Like it or loathe it, you cannot be indifferent to it. Now home to Warwick District Council, the building has been used for many purposes since its opening, including Friday night dances with no admittance after 9.45pm. Prior to 1974 Leamington's own council operated from here, employing its first female in 1929. The stonework was cleaned some years ago, but whether or not that was a good idea remains to be seen.

This end of the Parade had its share of well-known shops such as Boots the Chemist with its lending library as well as having books for sale. The ones from the library had large Boots stickers on them. Boots has now grown bigger and moved up town.

One of the longest lasting businesses was P H Woodward. The building was built in 1812 by C S Smith as the Upper Assembly Rooms, costing £10,000 and funded by local businessmen. The Rooms housed regular balls, concerts and public meetings with facilities for cards, billiards or just reading, all under the control of James Heaviside, the Master of Ceremonies. The venture was not a success and was sold at a loss. The building was taken over by P H Woodward in 1887, but this business has now sadly gone.

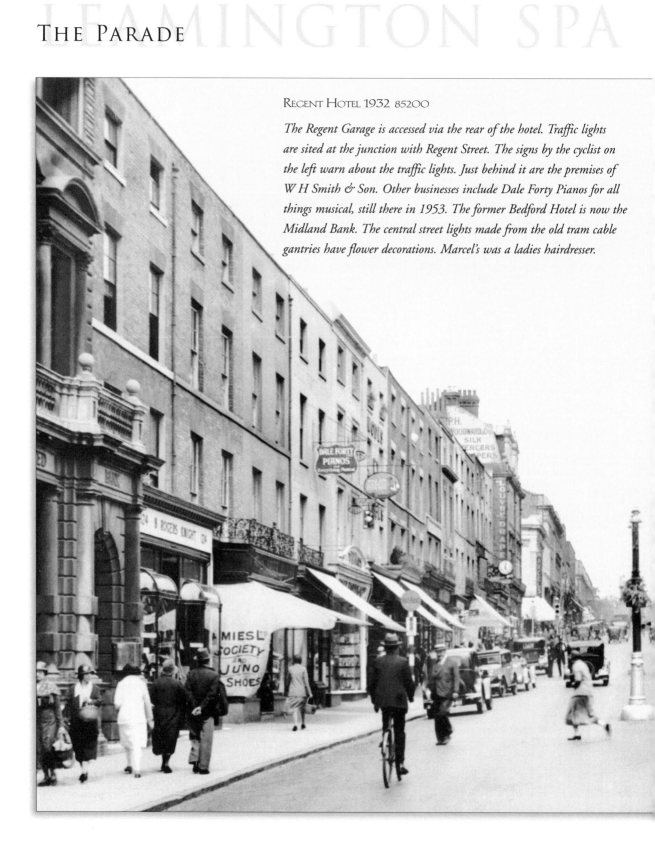

REGENT HOTEL 1932 85200

The Regent Garage is accessed via the rear of the hotel. Traffic lights are sited at the junction with Regent Street. The signs by the cyclist on the left warn about the traffic lights. Just behind it are the premises of W H Smith & Son. Other businesses include Dale Forty Pianos for all things musical, still there in 1953. The former Bedford Hotel is now the Midland Bank. The central street lights made from the old tram cable gantries have flower decorations. Marcel's was a ladies hairdresser.

THE PARADE

THE PARADE 1932 85204

The Chief Constable does not yet seem to have succeeded in ensuring that everyone drives on the left-hand side of the road! Left of Barclays Bank is Bobby's (centre), a top class store and restaurant — complete with resident orchestra. Later taken over by Debenhams, it is now owned by Lee Longland. Lipton's grocers, now gone, is another reminder of the days when foodshops had their place in town centres. Madame Duport sold confectionery as did her next door competitor, Savoury's, who also had a restaurant.

THE PARADE C1955 L25047D

P H Woodward was on the corner of the Parade and Regent Street and is now being rebuilt as contemporary luxery apartments. It seems only yesterday when they used a pneumatic tube system for sending money backwards and forwards to a central cashier, and then waited expectantly for the returned cannister to plop back into its basket. The Midland Red bus is a more modern design. Buses were used more then as car ownership had not yet recovered from the austerity of wartime. Freeman Hardy & Willis were one of the main shoe shops. What has the man by Woodward's got in his handcart? He is possibly a deliveryman or scrap metal collector.

LOWER PARADE & VICTORIA TERRACE

LOWER PARADE & VICTORIA TERRACE

STILL the main thoroughfare through Leamington, Lower Parade loses its straightness and curves away past the Town Hall towards the Royal Baths and Pump Room. In recent years some property has been rebuilt but it has retained its Regency style frontage. However, in many cases, shop windows can hardly be referred to similarly.

Traffic is far heavier and on-street parking is at a premium. Barclays Bank and HSBC Bank give a semblance of reassurance, but there is a regular turnover of retail businesses in the town. Fashions change over the years but the Parade is always thronged with people, especially at weekends.

Euston Place (or Estate Agents Row as it is more recently known), was named after a visitor to the town, but was sometimes called Union Promenade. It was built in 1838 - sadly, it burnt down the following year. It was rebuilt in its current form (but without the shop windows which were added later), completely altering the overall appearance of the buildings. Today it is the home of many of the town's estate agents.

THE PARADE C1955 L25078E

The ends of Regent Grove and Hamilton Terrace now have an attractive pedestrian refuge. Bunting is much in evidence - could it be for the coronation? The pseudo black and white building is the Haunch of Venison public house, now called The Lounge, - much used by the contestants at the annual Easter fencing competition held in the Town Hall. Left is the Cadena Café in front of which coffee beans were ground. Who can possibly forget that wonderful aroma!

LOWER PARADE & VICTORIA TERRACE

Above: THE PARADE 1892 30956

No motor vehicles ruin this genteel scene. Horse transport means no petrol pollution but problems of another kind! Hats, tail coats and full length dresses are the fashion. The trees, in full leaf, coupled with iron railings are very useful for tethering horses, especially when in the shade. No sunblinds are down so perhaps this is a Sunday. On the second storey above the second lamp post on the right, is where the Firemen's Statue once stood, prior to its removal to Euston Place. Gas lighting arrived in the Parade in 1823 at a cost of £63 to each household. The Royal Pump Room is situated on the right of the curve.

Left: LOWER PARADE 1932 85198

On the left at the corner of Dormer Place is the National Provincial Bank, now Pizza Express. Between the bank and Boots was Chocolate Lambert selling specially imported French chocolates. Today they would be Belgian. The staff worked long hours - from 9am to 8pm on weekdays and to 9pm on Saturdays. No heating was allowed for fear of melting the chocolates which were changed every day.

LOWER PARADE & VICTORIA TERRACE

Above: THE WAR MEMORIAL 1922 72447

The War Memorial was unveiled on 27 May 1922. Sadly many more names have been added from later wars. During the First World War a War Diary was kept in the local newspaper giving details of casualties etc. Rudyard Kipling's 'Tommy' was printed in full. There were appeals for cholera belts and pleas not to treat soldiers to drinks in pubs fearing it would cause drunkenness. Local vicars wrote sermons on the causes of the War. It was different in 1939 with blackout restrictions necessitating shops closing at 5pm during the winter months. Wooden rattles were to be sounded if poison gas was used. There was a quiet determination to get on with the job without all the patriotic fervour of 1914.

LOWER PARADE & VICTORIA TERRACE

On the premises of Locke & England is a statue of two firemen with a pump. Leamington had no fire brigade until 1856, when it became a police responsibility. Firemen were paid an extra three shillings a week on top of their police wages and one shilling for each call out. Any help from other brigades had to be paid for and a scale of attendance charges existed. There was a reluctance to call for help - having a fire was expensive.

Past the War Memorial the Parade straightens out and All Saints' Church becomes the most prominent feature, closely rivalled by the Royal Baths & Pump Room opposite Jephson Gardens.

In 1808-9 the existing bridge was widened as

THE PARADE & THE WAR MEMORIAL C1960 L25070

At the time of this photograph, ownership of motor cars was growing, especially with the introduction of the 'Moggy' (Morris) 1000 Traveller, which proved so popular it was even used by the police. Two telephone kiosks have sprouted on the corner of Euston Place. Most of the businesses have now either moved or disappeared and Martins Bank has long since been taken over.

Leamington expanded and it formed a vital link across the river for people wanting to access the new town to the north. By 1840 it needed renewing and J G Jackson was given the task. Renamed Victoria Bridge after the Queen, it was opened to commemorate her birthday. Dr Jephson performed the opening ceremony which was complete with a commemorative stone. Early next morning the stone was missing and was immediately reported as stolen. Then it re-appeared having been removed for safety during the night!

The Post Office originally began in Mill Street and moved to Beasley and Jones Chemists in Bath Street. Following a long struggle with the postal authorities to position it nearer the town centre, it was moved to

LOWER PARADE & VICTORIA TERRACE

Right: LOWER PARADE AND THE PARISH CHURCH
C1960 L25029

*Building work is taking place on the other side of
Boots, possibly at the National Provincial Bank. The
Schweppes delivery motor has no trouble driving up
town. A queue has gathered at the bus stop which has
some early parking regulations attached - no parking
for 10 yards either side of the stop.*

Above: THE PARADE C1955 L25078C

*Bunting is much in evidence. There is very little traffic
about although there are several parked cars. Bus design
still has not changed very much. The pillar box has
been moved, and is now probably the one on the corner
of Euston Place. A fascinating little car is driving in
splendid isolation up the Parade. The Gaiety is one
of several restaurants in Leamington now replaced by
other establishments.*

LOWER PARADE & VICTORIA TERRACE

Priory Terrace. Initially the upper floor was let to the Inland Revenue, but they moved out when the telephone exchange arrived.

The post arrived daily at midday and departed at 4.30pm, so the last post was effectively 4pm. In the 1890s the Post Office handled 170,000 letters and 5,500 parcels annually. Just over 100 years later the number of letters had risen to 345,000 per week. When first opened the Post Office had three members of staff, and by 1986 this had grown to 236 of all categories. 1971 saw the Post Office closed and moved across the road to Victoria Terrace as the building was planned for demolition. This was postponed and eight years later the Post Office returned to its old site and was officially re-opened.

In their blue frock coats, waistcoats and trousers, piped in scarlet, with scarlet collars and cuffs; low-brimmed hats with scarlet rim and gold coloured badges and buttons, the Victorian postmen would have added quite a splash of colour to the streets of Leamington.

On the other side of the road facing The Royal Pump Room on Victoria Bridge was the Tuscan-style Colonnade running along the river. In 1804 it housed Robbins Victoria Baths consisting of six marble baths and a small pump room. It was not a financial success and eventually closed. The Washington Hotel once stood on the corner. Another venture along the Colonnade was Heigler's Equestrian School, where Lockhart's Circus wintered. Its troupe entertained the town with parades. The building is no longer domed, and was at one time a skating rink.

When the Loft Theatre moved here in 1945 tip-up seats were brought over from Stratford in members' cars. 19 years later the Loft burnt down and today's theatre was built in its place. During the Second World War, part of the Colonnade was taken over by the Camouflage Department for the manufacture of nets and the like - or was it merely a front for more clandestine affairs?

Above Right: THE PARISH CHURCH FROM VICTORIA BRIDGE 1892 30963

The large building in front of the towerless All Saints' Parish Church is the Post Office, moved here in 1870. In front is a shelter where cabmen could rest between journeys. A cab waits outside, the horse tethered to a lamp post.

Right: VICTORIA TERRACE C1955 L25077B

The Post Office has not yet moved but the cabbies' shelter has gone. The central lamp posts are still ornate with floral decoration and Keep Left bollards have yet to be installed.

Far Right: VICTORIA TERRACE 1932 85211

The Colonnade makes an impressive entrance to the Loft Theatre. Note the traffic policeman, standing by the kerb on the right, wearing his white gloves.

From the Air

Taking the Waters

Until its demolition in 1960, spa water was always available here, with enamel mugs being chained to the wall for universal and totally unhealthy use. Today's environmental health people would surely have condemned such a practice. There was once a bicycle and tricycle shop adjoining the wellhouse and right in front of the church. To the right is the partial wording of 'Courier' indicating the premises of the local newspaper, further demonstrated by a hoarding board at the entrance to Church Walk.

TAKING THE WATERS

TAKING the waters in Leamington was not to be undertaken by the faint-hearted! Doing the job properly required stamina, with early morning starts and late night finishes. The season lasted from May to October and became a great social occasion for those who could afford it. There were two methods of treatment taken in conjunction with each other. Bathing should happen twice a week. Cold baths and tepid showers were available but without the severity experienced in Malvern.

To have any real effect, a 4-6 week course of drinking the mineral waters was recommended - the longer the better. Half a pint was taken first thing in the morning followed by 20 minutes' brisk exercise and then another half pint. For the best effect the water was drunk at the fountainhead. A full dose could induce drowsiness but this was quickly dispelled by walking or riding. Too much water made an effective laxative!

TAKING THE WATERS

ROYAL PUMP ROOM AND PARISH CHURCH 1922 72442

The little group pushing the pram with the girl on the scooter would not be sauntering leisurely along this part of the Parade today. She needs to take care her wheels do not lock into the tram lines. The Pump Rooms are on the right, complete with the tower which was later to be demolished. Turkish baths are available.

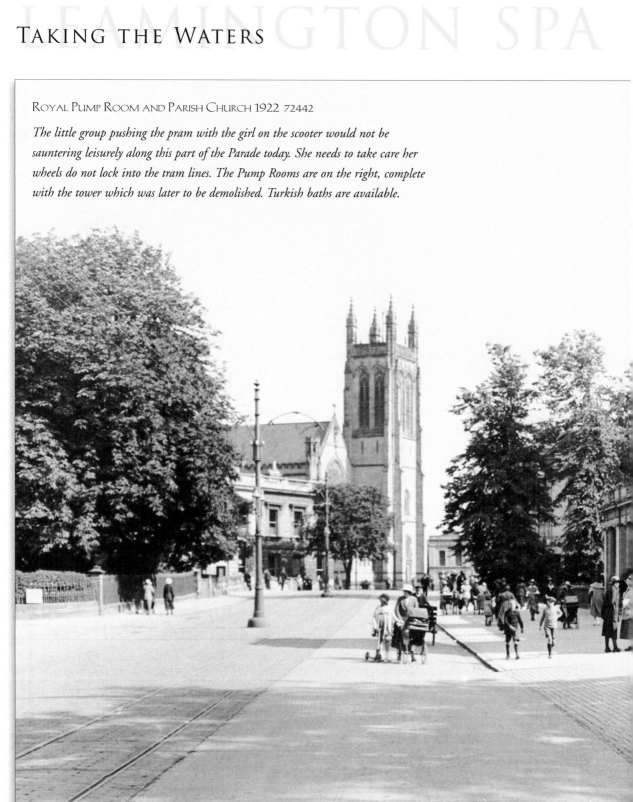

TAKING THE WATERS

ROYAL PUMP ROOM 1922 72443

The bathchair seen in this view from the opposite direction to 72442 (pages 40-41) shows that there were facilities for the disabled in the Baths. Riding bicycles and tricycles in the middle of the road between the tram lines seems to be the order of the day.

Far Left: THE PARADE C1950 L25046

Looking towards All Saints', the tram lines have gone and traffic remains sparse.

Left: THE ROYAL PUMP ROOM C1950 L25047B

By the 1950s Leamington was starting to lose its image of being solely for retired people. The many prams and bicycles indicate the growing presence of a younger generation.

However, there was much more than simply taking the waters. It became fashionable and other entertainments were provided. The local newspaper published names of the new arrivals and a whole host of hotels and inns clamoured for their patronage. In 1818 there were just six hotels in Leamington and only the Bedford was north of the river. Within two years this figure had doubled and by 1836 the town could boast 60 inns. Leamington became a popular social venue with widows and young ladies looking for husbands. They were well matched by fortune hunters seeking wealthy wives. All were helped in their respective hunts by monthly balls, theatres and soirées.

With the growth of Jephson Gardens further opportunities were provided for walking or indulging in archery and croquet. For the less energetic there was music from the bandstand in the Pump Room Gardens, initially of a military style but later more general. Cards, billiards and libraries all added to the available facilities.

The first recorded spa water in Leamington was discovered in 1586, some two years before the Spanish Armada. In 1803 the 4th Earl of Aylesford built over it. Two pipes carried the water, with one of them leading to the outside for free public access. For the wealthy there was a fixed scale of charges. It was used regularly and produced a considerable amount of revenue. Widow Webb, one of the earlier attendants, lived in a cottage at the corner of Church Walk. Here the original Spa Water Toffee was made. A later attendant used the well building as a bazaar for the sale of all manner of goods.

Although there were various pump rooms and water sources in Leamington, the only one to survive, albeit with difficulty, is the Royal Baths and Pump Room - usually referred to as the Pump Rooms. Designed by C S Smith of Warwick, they were built on land belonging to Bertie Greatheed. In 1813 a group of businessmen met and the idea of the Pump Rooms was born. No self-respecting spa town could be without one. The Pump Rooms opened for

43

PUMP ROOMS C1955 L25078B

From this view of the Pump Room we can ascertain that hats are still in fashion. Note the skirt lengths and the older 'Keep Left' bollards. The Linden Walk side of the Pump Rooms is covered. At the entrance to the swimming baths was a large map showing many Midlands' places of interest and here, from quite an early hour on a Sunday morning could be bought all kinds of newspapers and comics - an ideal arrangement for those going for an early swim. The tower was removed in 1953 during extensive rebuilding of the front.

business in 1814 although they would not be finished for another five years. A 2hp pump engine was installed by the engineer William Murdoch who invented gas lighting. A workman was injured during its installation. Some years later, a small chimney sweep became trapped in the flue and had to be rescued. The Pump Rooms were open from 7am to 3pm daily except Sundays, but success was not as immediate as the promoters would have wished.

Critics did not like its location alongside the River Leam with its evil colour, smell and scum. Fears were rampant about the possibility of contamination. Others did not like its cottage-like appearance although it would be rebuilt later. By 1860 its sale was suggested. The building was improved the following year just in time for the decline of inland spa towns. Further renovation took place and Turkish baths were added, as was a meteorological tower. However, long gone were the heady days when the Prince Regent visited and people took the waters.

In due course public baths were added. For the cost of one shilling the bath would be cleaned for you! 1890 saw the opening of the swimming baths, complete with wooden changing cubicles and hanging metal baskets for the swimmers to put their clothes in while they swam. Many a local child learnt to swim here. Somehow it is sad the baths have moved away from such a central town position.

The annexe was a 1910 addition. Behind the colonnade of Doric columns were the main Assembly Rooms. Here was a popular restaurant, complete with resident orchestra. There was a great uproar among the ladies

of Leamington when the last musicians were dismissed. There was even an item on the television news about it. In its heyday the restaurant was open daily except Christmas Day. The staff worked long hours with only one week's holiday. The Assembly Rooms were also available for private hire.

In 1964 a Regency Ball was held in the Pump Rooms to commemorate its 150th anniversary. Participants were encouraged to attend in period costume, which led to a heavy demand on local costume hirers. One young man found his breeches were such a bad fit that he was obliged to wear his mother's corsets in order to get into them, and then they had to be fixed with safety pins. For those arriving in costume, a horse and carriage service was provided from the Regent Hotel. It was superb arriving in style and seeing the envy in the eyes of spectators. Someone from the Regent Hotel was carried there in a sedan chair which unfortunately broke just past the Town Hall. It was a real night to remember.

The Pump Rooms remained in the care of Leamington Corporation until they were taken over by Warwick District Council in 1974. More renovation was needed and the medical wing was closed in 1990 and transferred to the Warneford Hospital. It was a short stay as the hospital was demolished in 1993 and they returned to the Pump Rooms. The whole complex was closed in 1997 and has been extensively rebuilt and refurbished. Spa water can be obtained here. When the Pump Rooms were opened their title was changed to The Royal Baths and Pump Room. However the title to be seen today and which appears in these pictures is Royal Pump Room and Baths!

JEPHSON GARDENS

JEPHSON GARDENS, THE ENTRANCE 1892 30968

The Gatehouses, designed in Italianate style by Squirhill, were built specifically to flank the entrance.
A maximum height of 30 feet was agreed so as not to overshadow the Pump Rooms. They were used
to house the Gardens' Superintendent and his office. Replacement gates were fitted in 1948. Notice
boards advertise concerts etc in the gardens. The original bandstand was moved following complaints
about the noise. Police officers were allowed to enter the gardens only in the course of their duties, and
not just to listen to the music.

JEPHSON GARDENS

UNDOUBTEDLY one of Leamington's most famous features, the gardens were named after Dr Henry Jephson who helped put Leamington on the map. He was a much respected doctor whose patients included Queen Victoria and Florence Nightingale. The gardens were originally for the benefit of the residents of adjacent Newbold Terrace but in 1846 Dr Jephson acquired them for all to enjoy. The land belonged to Edward Willes who leased it to the town for a peppercorn rent over a period of not less than 2,000 years. Their official opening was heralded by continuous bell ringing and a half mile-long procession ending in the gardens with some 7,000 people in attendance. The gardens were re-opened in 2003, in the presence of members of the Jephson family, following extensive renovation.

Dr John Hitchman was a firm believer in hydrotherapeutic treatment and had his own private clinic called the Arboretum which had 40 beds and 40 acres of grounds for patients. In 1846 he donated money towards the formal laying out of Jephson Gardens with the proviso that the work must be carried out by the local unemployed. He also gave £8,000 towards improving the Pump Rooms. He died in 1867.

The gardens, laid out in a formal style, are a showpiece. In the past they included an aviary and small menagerie which have now gone. The only animal life there now is natural, such as swans, geese and ducks. Jephson's Temple in the background became a popular place for official group pictures.

The wide-pathed formality of the gardens is very apparent today yet has an ever-changing pattern of garden and flower beds. Over the years, many plants and trees have been donated in someone's memory. One such remembers Henry Tandy VC DCM MM who was one of the most highly-decorated privates of the First World War. Local tradition always believed he had saved the life of Adolf Hitler during an incident. Other sources now cast doubt on this claim.

JEPHSON GARDENS

For years the gardens were illuminated for evening visitors by small candles in jars. After the austere years of the Second World War, the Lights of Leamington became a major attraction during the summer months with visitors coming by the coachload. Themes changed annually and the lights became more sophisticated. Candles in jars were replaced by electricity. Time switches gave the impression of jumping rabbits or other animals. Disney characters came and went - as did the crowds. It was a popular event, albeit never on the same scale as Blackpool.

In 1968 the Czech Fountain was added near Jephson's Temple. It is in the shape of a parachute, with the water forming its strings, and between each channel are the names of the members of the Czechoslavak Brigade who, in 1942, parachuted into Prague and assassinated the Nazi Reichsprotektor, SS Obergruppenfuehrer Reinhard Heydrich. The operation was planned in a nearby house, now demolished, in Newbold Terrace. Nearby is a Rose Garden dedicated to the memory of the villagers of Liddice and Lasaky who were massacred by the Nazis in retaliation.

Below: ENTRANCE TO JEPHSON GARDENS 1922 72457

This view dates from 40 years later than 30968 (pages 46-47) and the front is still immaculate. The gates now have a name over the top. Regular Corporation concerts are advertised. The riverside pavilion was in constant use until 1973. Electric trams pass the gates with their overhead gantries doubling up as street lights.

JEPHSON GARDENS

JEPHSON GARDENS C1955 L25034
John Cundall's memorial fountain to Dr Hitchman stands on the corner of the gardens flanked by Lower Parade and Newbold Terrace. It is built on the site of Strawberry Cottage, but does not always work because fallen leaves often block the jets.

Above Left: JEPHSON GARDENS ENTRANCE 1932 85206

Ten years after 72457 and the trams have gone. The entrance is a popular waiting place. This was the recent site of the controversial soup kitchen which was moved to a less sensitive site causing much bitterness in the process.

Above Right: JEPHSON GARDENS TEMPLE 1892 30967

Edward Willes probably felt somewhat slighted when a statue of Dr Jephson by Peter Hollins was erected in this temple in 1846, after all he had given the land to the town and not Dr Jephson. Some years ago the statue lost a hand. It was suggested by a visiting American who knew the story, that the damage had been caused by Edward Willes's ghost getting his revenge!

JEPHSON GARDENS, THE LAKE 1922 72459

Constructed in 1846, the lake became popular with families. Fountainless, it was an ideal place to sail model yachts or just to be enjoyed by strolling past. The obelisk memorial is to Edward Willes and was erected in 1875. It is not as grandiose as Jephson's Temple, but is a memorial all the same.

JEPHSON GARDENS

JEPHSON GARDENS 1922 72466

This path has changed little over the years. Hats are still very much obligatory for both sexes.

JEPHSON GARDENS

JEPHSON GARDENS C1960 L25060

The mushroom-shaped objects in the flower beds are probably part of the illuminations. One year there was an Emmett Clock which played the Blue Danube several times a day and put quite a strain on locals' love of classical music. The Lights of Leamington have faded into memories, but they played an important part in helping the Midlands return to normal after the war years. The wooden hut is possibly something to do with the maintenance of the gardens.

JEPHSON GARDENS C1960 L25076

The fountains arrived in 1925 and are based on the ones at Hampton Court. They caused model yachts to give way to ducks and swans since they were unable to cope with such choppy conditions. In the late 1940s going to feed the ducks in the Gardens was an exciting treat for a small child. In a severe winter the lake froze and became a big attraction for children and skaters of all ages. The park keeper would send everybody off but once he had gone they probably all returned. For safety reasons, the lake has now been fenced off to restrict access to the water, except for the wildlife.

ENTERTAINMENT

THE RIVER LEAM rises in the county of Northamptonshire and is the main waterway through Leamington, joining the Avon at Portobello. Today the river is comparitively clean but in Victorian times raw sewage was thrown into it. Whilst the Leam is not particularly deep it can and does flood quite disastrously. The last time was in 1998 when it inundated Jephson Gardens, the Parade and neighbouring houses. The damage done by the floods left people with deep feelings of misery and hurt over the way they felt they were treated by the various authorities.

Boats and water go together and in spite of the sewage, Leamington has been no exception. Rowing boats, later followed by motor boats and canoes have all had their day. Sadly, most of them no longer exist. To take a canoe out on a summer's evening was an enjoyable experience. Upriver was not quite so easy and tended to be mainly around the Mill Gardens and the Upper Leam through countryside. The weirs are big hazards to navigation and effectively form the natural limits to it. There were some lock facilities but they have fallen into disuse over the last 100 years or so. The river was just the place to take the ladies, possibly with a picnic aboard. Now the river tends to be used mainly by the local canoe club or sea scouts.

BOAT HOUSE 1892 30978

Such river scenes as this are highly evocative of the Victorian love of boating, epitomised in 'Three Men in a Boat' and 'Wind in the Willows'. This photo could be well summed up by the expression 'messing about on the river'.

ENTERTAINMENT

The advent of the railway played its part in bringing visitors to the town and taking them away! The line between Coventry and Leamington passes by Victoria Park and was once part of the LMS network.

Not all visitors wished to partake in strenuous exercise and many sought less energetic pastimes, such as going to the theatre. In time theatres gave way to being cinemas, then became bingo halls or were put to other uses. The Leamington Theatre Company was founded in 1881. The Theatre Royal was built by John Fell at a cost of £10,000. Sadly six months later it went bankrupt. After its re-opening bad luck struck repeatedly. One of the more successful owners was Mr Watson Mill who took over in 1921. In 1935 the Theatre became the Regent Cinema complete with organ. The downward cycle continued and 40 years later it became a bingo hall before finally being demolished. The site now houses part of Regent Court and is a mixture of restaurants, car park and residential apartments.

In the 1950s cinemas had an irritating habit of showing a film with a 'U' or Universal certificate with a supporting film with an 'A' or 'Accompanied by an Adult' certificate. In order to get round this in the absence of parents, the usual practice was for the unaccompanied youngster to ask other adults in the queue to take him or her in with them. Once inside, the adults and children would go their own ways. Imagine trying to do that today. Another trick was to buy a ticket for the cheapest seats, usually in front of a thick white line and then, after the lights went out, surreptitiously move back to a better seat.

JEPHSON GARDENS c1960 L25036

Here we see the famous swaying suspension bridge built in 1903. To the right of the bridge are two of the sluice tunnels for use in floods. To their right is the site of one of the town's watermills. Right of that, between the bridge and trees, is Elephant Walk, where circus elephants were taken to drink and bathe. On the left is the edge of Jephson Gardens complete with motor boats for hire.

ENTERTAINMENT

Above: THEATRE AND REGENT GROVE 1922 72441

The trees on the left once formed part of a private drive to Newbold Comyn House (now demolished) and were given to the town by Edward Willes. Almost opposite the Theatre stood a Crimean War cannon until it was melted down for the early 1940s war effort. Mr Watson Mill would have been the manager for this production of 'The Musical Romance'.

Opposite Top: ADELAIDE BRIDGE 1892 30979

Seen here after its re-building by William de Normanville in 1891. Leamington has four bridges across the river. It is easy to imagine punts or rowing boats passing, powered by men in flannel trousers, striped blazers and straw boaters!

Opposite Bottom: RAILWAY BRIDGE 1892 30985

We are looking back towards Leamington showing the weir, an outer limit for boaters. The viaduct carries the Milverton extension of the railway. Behind the viaduct is Victoria Park, site of the old open-air swimming baths which had such a slippery bottom that only boys were allowed to use them. To the right is now the Princes Drive Waste Disposal Centre, known locally as 'the tip'. Princes Bridge, between the weir and the viaduct, was not built until 1923.

Other less energetic pastimes involved the gentle art of sitting or strolling in one of the parks. The Royal Pump Room Gardens were situated alongside the Pump Rooms but were not available for public use until 1889. Previously Linden Avenue had been fenced off to keep the common people away. Here the better off could sit and enjoy their picnics or afternoon tea, properly waited on of course, whilst the less fortunate looked on. The trees were planted in 1828 as part of Leamington's expansion. They were funded by a grand bazaar held in the Pump Rooms.

Leamington has two distinctions when it comes to tennis. Firstly it has one of the few Real Tennis courts in the country. Secondly it is where the first lawn tennis match was played. Lawn tennis was invented by Birmingham solicitor Harry Gem and Spanish merchant Augurio Perera. Their first experiments took place in Edgbaston before they moved to Leamington.

ROYAL PUMP ROOM GARDENS 1922 72471

This shows a similar view to 72470 (page 13) but from the vicinity of the Pump Rooms. It is a typical summer's day as evidenced by the umbrellas and coats! However nothing is going to spoil the concert. St Peter's Church is to the left.

ENTERTAINMENT

LINDEN AVENUE 1922 72475

Once known as the Monkey Run, the barriers here came down in 1875. The crowns and arches were added in 1887 and a large gas lamp hung from each one. The Pump Rooms, All Saints' Church and the Jephson Gardens Lodge Gates are plainly visible.

ROYAL PUMP ROOM GARDENS 1922 72470

This photograph was taken from across the river near the Manor House Hotel. The Bandstand is the prominent feature. The wide paths between the flower beds enable bicycles, prams and bathchairs to pass each other comfortably.

MANOR HOUSE HOTEL 1892 30977

This was once the home of Matthew Wise and dates back to 1780. The bulk of the building is High Victorian Gothic and has been used as a hotel since the 1840s. Its main claim to fame is being the site of the first lawn tennis match held here in 1872. The actual site is now covered by the adjoining Manor Court Flats. The fountain was added late in the 19th century. Opposite the hotel was the tram terminus. Whilst the hotel has now closed, extensive building work has been undertaken at the rear, and the whole site is now home to 66 apartments.

AN ORDNANCE SURVEY MAP SHOWING LEAMINGTON SPA AND SURROUNDING AREAS 1886

RELIGION

WORSHIP plays an important part in community life and Leamington is no exception, although many of its churches and chapels are redundant or even demolished. For Christians the 19th century was a period of great revival. It was a time when some vicars actually owned their churches or had paid for them to be built and rival churches could be established in the same parish. Nevertheless this period typified Leamington's religious growth. Climb any high spot in Leamington or Warwick and see how the spires stick out above the roofline in every direction. It is difficult to accept that at one time there were even more.

St Alban's Church was built in 1864 and demolished in 1964. Its green copper spire earned it the nickname of the Mouldy Cheese steeple. Originally sited in Priory Terrace where it was known as the Iron Church or, more correctly, the Church of St Michael and All Angels. Being so close to All Saints' Church it was also known as the New Opposition Church.

St Mark's Church 1892 30957

The church was built in Gothic Revival style by George Gilbert Scott in 1879. St Mark's dominates the Rugby Road approach to Leamington. It had a hard task replacing the old Milverton Episcopal Chapel, fondly known as the Pepperbox. Lively in detail, especially at the top of the spire, the church interior was typical of Scott's work, with lozenge-shaped pillars into which arches sank. The stained glass window in the chancel is by Kempe. The Reverend Charles Carus-Wilson bore the costs and was to have been the vicar, but sadly died before the building was completed. In this picture of the church the action seems to be at the far end of the road with a few handcarts and an open carriage, possibly a cab. The nearest vehicle seems to be a carriage of sorts.

It was erected on the site of a garden belonging to Orleans House, now the Conservative Club, and was purchased by the Reverend John Craig, vicar of All Saints'. He ensured the church was entirely self-supporting without any help whatever from All Saints'.

Christ Church was another victim of demolition in spite of holding such a prominent position at the top of the Parade. One of the more fascinating examples of ecclesiastical architecture in Leamington, its demolition was nothing short of legal vandalism. All that remains now of such a unique church are Christchurch Gardens. Trees grow where the church once stood.

The church was built in 1825 in the Norman Revival style, also known as Pure Saxon, by P F Robinson of London. The land was presented by Bertie Greatheed, but ultimately the church found itself heavily in debt. One way of raising money was to charge people to go to church - 6d for visitors but half price for servants. This idea was scrapped in 1839 after the church was purchased by the Reverend John Craig.

ST PAUL'S CHURCH 1922 72451

This photograph is a street scene showing typical late 19th-century urban building. St Paul's Church, on the other side of Leamington to St Mark's, has a 150 feet high spire. It was designed in brick by John Cundall and opened in 1874. Consecration did not take place for a further four years until the tower had been built.

CHRIST CHURCH c1955 L25021

The road in this picture remains the A452 but the priority of the junction has altered. Bus shelters tend to get vandalised and so have been removed.

ST ALBAN'S CHURCH 1892 30958

Plenty of iron railings can be seen here. The tram lines run along here on the way to Warwick.

The philosophy behind Christ Church was simplicity, with simple services and a hand-blown organ. Vicars were obliged not to wear their surplices in the pulpit and the pre-sermon hymns were extra long to allow time for their removal.

Christ Church was demolished in 1959 on a thick foggy day as if its demise was to be hidden from witnesses. The contractors had to borrow a ladder from the Fire Brigade to reach the tower.

As Leamington grew, more Roman Catholics came into the town. Their services were no longer banned and the problem was finding big enough premises. So St Peter's was born. Designed by Henry Clutton,

it was erected between 1861-5 and opened in 1864 before it had been completed. The tower, known as the Pineapple Tower, was added in 1872.

Disaster struck five years later. Work had been carried out in the organ loft where a candle had been left burning and, as a consequence, the tower caught fire. The Fire Brigade, then a police responsibility, tried in vain to stop it but the water jets did not have the power to reach the blaze. Onlookers are reputed to have declined to assist with the hand pumping. The damage amounted to £6-8,000 and both Protestants and Roman Catholics contributed to the restoration fund. Then in 1903 the tower was found to be unsafe and had to be reconstructed.

All Saints' is the largest church in Warwickshire and a far cry from the earlier building started over 900 years ago. The continual extension of the church ceased to be practical and J C Jackson was given the task of rebuilding it. He was very much his own man and believed in the Continental Gothic style. The rebuilding commenced in 1843 under the Reverend John Craig and finished in 1869. The tower was added between 1898-1902.

John Craig was an Irishman who married well. He gave liberally to good causes and was the driving force behind the re-building. In the process he upset many people who tried, unsuccessfully, to have him removed. He remained in office for 38 years.

Spencer Street Chapel is redundant and now used as a carpet showroom. No doubt its founders would be horrified! The foundation stone was laid in 1836 when this part of town was still countryside. The Chapel originated when the congregation grew too big for its existing building in Clemens Street. 1849 saw a split in the congregation and part of it moved to Holly Walk.

ROYAL PUMP ROOM GARDENS 1932 85208

St Peter's dominates the skyline. This picture is taken ten years after 72471 (pages 60-61). More deck chairs are in use but with plenty of room for more. Are people just milling about, enjoying the sunshine, or waiting for a concert to begin? No doubt the park keepers know.

RELIGION

ALL SAINTS' CHURCH 1892 30961

This magnificent view shows the church before the tower was added. On the right is Camden's Well. At the side, Church Walk leads into the churchyard, passing the offices of The Courier. Perhaps the pony and trap are carrying milk or bread - provisions were still delivered in this fashion in the 1950s. The tram is a lovely example of the horse-drawn service before it was electrified in 1905. It seems to be moving more slowly than the pony and trap. Note the advertisement on its side for the Bedford Stores run by Messrs Burgis & Colbourne. On the left is the corner of Harris's Victoria Stores, a wonderful old-fashioned grocery store which existed well into the 1950s. It was a place with a feast of smells and all manner of produce waiting to be weighed and bagged.

Opposite Top: SPENCER STREET 1932 85212

The Chapel is on the left with its Palladian style Greek Doric columns - another example of Squirhill's work. Opposite is the old Clifton Cinema and car showrooms. The Clifton is now Evolve Nightclub and Gymnasium, whilst the car showrooms are empty and available to rent.

Opposite Bottom: PARISH CHURCH C1955 L25039

The churchyard, giving a good view of the great rose window similar to that at St Ouen at Rouen.

Below: PARISH CHURCH C1955 L25078A

Coats are in fashion although the wearing of hats is not so popular. Bunting is flying down the centre of the Parade.

LEAMINGTON SPA

RELIGION

The chapel vaults housed the town's first Nonconformist school for boys with an attendance record of 80%. The children had no playground. A flight of steps ran down from the outside of the building into the school. During winter there was a tiny grate, about two feet wide, to give a meagre heat. Two windows on the outside wall gave some light, but only 18 inches of them were above ground. A new school was built in 1856 overlooking the graveyard, still with no playground although it was light and airy. Its inaugural Christmas Concert raised enough money to start a library of 500-600 books.

With Leamington steadily expanding into the countryside, it was inevitable that public buildings would follow. St Mary's and St John's Churches are such examples. Built in 15th-century Ecclesiastical style by J C Jackson in 1839, St Mary's struggled for existence; John Craig was firmly against the idea of having another church inside his parish. When built St Mary's was surrounded by open fields, many belonging to Edward Willes. Today the church is well inside the town. On John Craig's death in 1877, St Mary's became a parish in its own right.

THE RIVER LEAM 1922 72436

The River Leam and All Saints' Church from the suspension bridge. On the left, the high walls at the rear of the gardens give an indication of the flood problems associated with living on a river.

Mrs Hitchman, widow of Dr Hitchman, donated the site for this church together with a large sum of money. St Mary's was built between 1877 and 1878 by John Cundall in brick with a prominent steeple. The interior is brick-lined. The tower was a mere 75 feet high and has been cemented over. In 1875 the old three-decker pulpit was removed and the font re-located. The horse and carriage gives a tranquil atmosphere on a road which now leads to an industrial estate.

ST JOHN'S CHURCH, TATCHBROOK ROAD 1892 30989

The church was built on land where Dr Hitchman once had his clinic. Today's road is far busier than shown here.

St Mark's Church

OUT OF TOWN

LEAMINGTON'S only known windmill remained a popular landmark on the Tachbrook Road until its demolition in 1968. Once a popular subject for postcards, especially in a wintry scene, its only reminder now is in the nearby Windmill pub, enlarged and modernised in 1986, and a housing estate. In 1926 the Leamington Slum Clearance Company set up as a registered charity and built this estate as one of its many projects.

There was a proposal to extend the tramway to Whitnash, which was a quiet village outside the town. Nathaniel Hawthorne wrote about the village in his book, 'Our Old Home'. He describes Whitnash as a typical English village. Of Roman origins, Whitnash has changed dramatically in recent years and Hawthorne would have difficulty in recognising it. At the time of the Domesday Book it had a population of 112. About 150 years ago

TACHBROOK ROAD WINDMILL 1892 30987

Today Tachbrook Road bears no resemblance to this gentle rural scene over 100 years ago. The area opposite the Windmill and behind the trees was to become the major industrial premises of Lockheed. The building to the left of the windmill is the pub of the same name.

OUT OF TOWN

it had more trees than houses and no real roads. Access was by paths, lanes and cultivated fields. By the time of the time of the 2001 Census, the population had risen to 7,798. Today Whitnash is a town in its own right, complete with mayor and council.

St Margaret of Antioch is the patron saint of this church (and also of women in childbirth). Restoration work began in 1855 and lasted some years. It included the addition of a stone pulpit. Commemorated inside is

Rector Nicholas Greenhill, First Master at Rugby School and Captain of Foot in the Royalist Army at Oxford. Also remembered is Benedict Medley, Clerk to the Signet of Henry VII and Lord of the Manor.

Whitnash's village green was an important focal point of rural life. Here the rectory cricket team played in the 1860s, where the stocks had once stood, and in 1872 Joseph Arch, that great agricultural trade unionist, addressed a strike meeting there.

WHITNASH VILLAGE 1892 30990

The Plough and Harrow still stands here although the road lay-out is very different. This is a tranquil scene with some of the half-timbered buildings still standing, but today's pedestrians are recommended not to stand about in the road like this!

WHITNASH VILLAGE 1892 30991

A scene which sums up late Victorian rural England. Is this a school group with their teacher? The school was opened by Henry Landor in 1860. In the distance is St Margaret's Church. Originally Saxon, it was re-built by Sir George Gilbert Scott.

Out of Town

WHITNASH, ST MARGARET'S
CHURCH 1922 72485

*The old storm-damaged elm tree
outside the church was removed
in 1960 for safety reasons, causing
considerable difference of opinion
between the county authorities and
the locals. For many years it had
been an important symbol in local
fertility rites. Its removal brought
quite groundless fears of there being
no more babies in Whitnash!*

WHITNASH VILLAGE 1922 72483

The war memorial was dedicated in 1920. The shops on the left are a poignant reminder of a vanishing way of village life. Today's environmental health people would be aghast at the old practice of bakers putting their bread out on the green to cool!

NAMES OF SUBSCRIBERS

The following people have kindly supported this book by purchasing limited edition copies prior to publication.

Andrew Beckett

The Bicknell Family, Leamington Spa

A tribute to our dad, Vincent Broughton

Dorothy Carroll, Royal Leamington Spa

Les & Jean Clarkson, Whitnash

Ellen Anne Clifton

The Crawford family, Cubbington

Ernie Critten 2006, Leamington Spa

Alan Crossan, Leamington Spa

Marion Crossan, Leamington Spa

In memory of Helen and Tom Croy

Mr and Mrs R Dodd

To Laurence Ell, with love from all your family

Frank J Ferriday

John Richard Fisher, Royal Leamington Spa

The Fitzmaurice Family

Elisabeth Forrest

Linda Forth on her Birthday

To the Garners of Wasperton Hill Farm

The Gascoigne Family, Whitnash

To Pam, in memory of Fred and Elsie Giles

The Graham Family

Maurice and Vilma Green, Whitnash

The Hajarnavis Family, Cubbington

Roy Halford, 17th July 1940, Leamington Spa

To Barry Harwood, on his 65th birthday

For our parents, Anthony and Yvonne Hawkins

Des and Deirdre Hayward

In memory of P Hiley, Leamington Spa

The Hodgkins Family, Whitnash

Joy and Len Hunt, Gary and Janice

Barry Ives and family

Mr N A K Kitchen, with love from your parents

Mr M A Kitchen, with love from your parents

For Freddi, dear friend of Alan and Marion

A tribute to my parents, R and E Mann

Jill Elizabeth Marchant of Leamington Spa

In memory of Vernon May

Jim Nason, Kenilworth

Paul Nason

Lesley Nason

Kenneth Owen

To our son, Sean Pearcey, love Mum and Dad

In memory of Bill and Bessie Potter

The Shayler Family, sons Phil, Doug and Malcolm

In loving memory of Muriel Simmons

Michael J Smith, Old Leamingtonian

Gillian and Robert Starkey, Whitnash

Janet & John Statham

Paul and Linda Stoodley and Anthony, Whitnash

To Tony, love Mum and Dad

In memory of Peter Alan Turrell

Henry James Ward, Blacksmith, Leamington

Nick, Lesley, Tom, Toria Whiting

Mrs Susan Williams, Leamington Spa

To Grandad Derek Willoughby on his 70th

www.francisfrith.com

The Francis Frith Collection publishes over 100 new titles each year. A selection of those currently available is listed below. For latest catalogue please contact The Francis Frith Collection. **Town Books** 96 pages, approximately 75 photos. **County and Themed Books** 128 pages, approximately 135 photos (unless specified). Pocket Albums are miniature editions of Frith local history books 128 pages, approximately 95 photos.

Accrington Old and New
Alderley Edge and Wilmslow
Amersham, Chesham and Rickmansworth
Andover
Around Abergavenny
Around Alton
Aylesbury
Barnstaple
Bedford
Bedfordshire
Berkshire Living Memories
Berkshire Pocket Album
Blackpool Pocket Album
Bognor Regis
Bournemouth
Bradford
Bridgend
Bridport
Brighton and Hove
Bristol
Buckinghamshire
Calne Living Memories
Camberley Pocket Album
Canterbury Cathedral
Cardiff Old and New
Chatham and the Medway Towns
Chelmsford
Chepstow Then and Now
Cheshire
Cheshire Living Memories
Chester
Chesterfield
Chigwell
Christchurch
Churches of East Cornwall
Clevedon
Clitheroe
Corby Living Memories
Cornish Coast
Cornwall Living Memories
Cotswold Living Memories
Cotswold Pocket Album
Coulsdon, Chipstead and Woodmanstern
County Durham
Cromer, Sheringham and Holt
Dartmoor Pocket Album
Derby
Derbyshire
Derbyshire Living Memories
Devon
Devon Churches
Dorchester

Dorset Coast Pocket Album
Dorset Living Memories
Dorset Villages
Down the Dart
Down the Severn
Down the Thames
Dunmow, Thaxted and Finchingfield
Durham
East Anglia Pocket Album
East Devon
East Grinstead
Edinburgh
Ely and The Fens
Essex Pocket Album
Essex Second Selection
Essex: The London Boroughs
Exeter
Exmoor
Falmouth
Farnborough, Fleet and Aldershot
Folkestone
Frome
Furness and Cartmel Peninsulas
Glamorgan
Glasgow
Glastonbury
Gloucester
Gloucestershire
Greater Manchester
Guildford
Hailsham
Hampshire
Harrogate
Hastings and Bexhill
Haywards Heath Living Memories
Heads of the Valleys
Heart of Lancashire Pocket Album
Helston
Herefordshire
Horsham
Humberside Pocket Album
Huntingdon, St Neots and St Ives
Hythe, Romney Marsh and Ashford
Ilfracombe
Ipswich Pocket Album
Isle of Wight
Isle of Wight Living Memories
King's Lynn
Kingston upon Thames
Lake District Pocket Album
Lancashire Living Memories
Lancashire Villages

Available from your local bookshop or from the publisher

The Francis Frith Collection Titles (continued)

Lancaster, Morecambe and Heysham Pocket Album
Leeds Pocket Album
Leicester
Leicestershire
Lincolnshire Living Memoires
Lincolnshire Pocket Album
Liverpool and Merseyside
London Pocket Album
Ludlow
Maidenhead
Maidstone
Malmesbury
Manchester Pocket Album
Marlborough
Matlock
Merseyside Living Memories
Nantwich and Crewe
New Forest
Newbury Living Memories
Newquay to St Ives
North Devon Living Memories
North London
North Wales
North Yorkshire
Northamptonshire
Northumberland
Northwich
Nottingham
Nottinghamshire Pocket Album
Oakham
Odiham Then and Now
Oxford Pocket Album
Oxfordshire
Padstow
Pembrokeshire
Penzance
Petersfield Then and Now
Plymouth
Poole and Sandbanks
Preston Pocket Album
Ramsgate Old and New
Reading Pocket Album
Redditch Living Memories
Redhill to Reigate
Richmond
Ringwood
Rochdale
Romford Pocket Album
Salisbury Pocket Album
Scotland
Scottish Castles
Sevenoaks and Tonbridge
Sheffield and South Yorkshire Pocket Album
Shropshire
Somerset
South Devon Coast
South Devon Living Memories
South East London
Southampton Pocket Album
Southend Pocket Album
Southport

Southwold to Aldeburgh
Stourbridge Living Memories
Stratford upon Avon
Stroud
Suffolk
Suffolk Pocket Album
Surrey Living Memories
Sussex
Sutton
Swanage and Purbeck
Swansea Pocket Album
Swindon Living Memories
Taunton
Teignmouth
Tenby and Saundersfoot
Tiverton
Torbay
Truro
Uppingham
Villages of Kent
Villages of Surrey
Villages of Sussex Pocket Album
Wakefield and the Five Towns Living Memories
Warrington
Warwick
Warwickshire Pocket Album
Wellingborough Living Memories
Wells
Welsh Castles
West Midlands Pocket Album
West Wiltshire Towns
West Yorkshire
Weston-super-Mare
Weymouth
Widnes and Runcorn
Wiltshire Churches
Wiltshire Living Memories
Wiltshire Pocket Album
Wimborne
Winchester Pocket Album
Windermere
Windsor
Wirral
Wokingham and Bracknell
Woodbridge
Worcester
Worcestershire
Worcestershire Living Memories
Wyre Forest
York Pocket Album
Yorkshire
Yorkshire Coastal Memories
Yorkshire Dales
Yorkshire Revisited

See Frith books on the internet at www.francisfrith.com

FRITH PRODUCTS & SERVICES

Francis Frith would doubtless be pleased to know that the pioneering publishing venture he started in 1860 still continues today. Over a hundred and forty years later, The Francis Frith Collection continues in the same innovative tradition and is now one of the foremost publishers of vintage photographs in the world. Some of the current activities include:

Interior Decoration

Today Frith's photographs can be seen framed and as giant wall murals in thousands of pubs, restaurants, hotels, banks, retail stores and other public buildings throughout the country. In every case they enhance the unique local atmosphere of the places they depict and provide reminders of gentler days in an increasingly busy and frenetic world.

Product Promotions

Frith products are used by many major companies to promote the sales of their own products or to reinforce their own history and heritage. Frith promotions have been used by Hovis bread, Courage beers, Scots Porage Oats, Colman's mustard, Cadbury's foods, Mellow Birds coffee, Dunhill pipe tobacco, Guinness, and Bulmer's Cider.

Genealogy and Family History

As the interest in family history and roots grows world-wide, more and more people are turning to Frith's photographs of Great Britain for images of the towns, villages and streets where their ancestors lived; and, of course, photographs of the churches and chapels where their ancestors were christened, married and buried are an essential part of every genealogy tree and family album.

Frith Products

All Frith photographs are available Framed or just as Mounted Prints and Posters (size 23 x 16 inches). These may be ordered from the address below. From time to time other products - Address Books, Calendars, Table Mats, etc - are available.

The Internet

Already ninety thousand Frith photographs can be viewed and purchased on the internet through the Frith websites and a myriad of partner sites.

For more detailed information on Frith companies and products, look at this site:

www.francisfrith.com

See the complete list of Frith Books at:
www.francisfrith.com
This web site is regularly updated with the latest list of publications from The Francis Frith Collection. If you wish to buy books relating to another part of the country that your local bookshop does not stock, you may purchase on-line.

For further information, trade, or author enquiries please contact us at the address below:
The Francis Frith Collection, Frith's Barn, Teffont, Salisbury, Wiltshire, England SP3 5QP.
Tel: +44 (0)1722 716 376   Fax: +44 (0)1722 716 881   Email: sales@francisfrith.co.uk

---

See Frith books on the internet at www.francisfrith.com

FREE PRINT OF YOUR CHOICE

Mounted Print
Overall size 14 x 11 inches (355 x 280mm)

Choose any Frith photograph in this book.
Simply complete the Voucher opposite and return it with your remittance for £3.50 (to cover postage and handling) and we will print the photograph of your choice in SEPIA (size 11 x 8 inches) and supply it in a cream mount with a burgundy rule line (overall size 14 x 11 inches). **Please note: photographs with a reference number starting with a "Z" are not Frith photographs and cannot be supplied under this offer.
Offer valid for delivery to one UK address only.**

PLUS: Order additional Mounted Prints at HALF PRICE - £7.49 each (normally £14.99)
If you would like to order more Frith prints from this book, possibly as gifts for friends and family, you can buy them at half price (with no additional postage and handling costs).

PLUS: Have your Mounted Prints framed
For an extra £14.95 per print you can have your mounted print(s) framed in an elegant polished wood and gilt moulding, overall size 16 x 13 inches (no additional postage and handling required).

IMPORTANT!

These special prices are only available if you use this form to order. You must use the ORIGINAL VOUCHER on this page (no copies permitted). We can only despatch to one UK address. This offer cannot be combined with any other offer.

Send completed Voucher form to:
The Francis Frith Collection, Frith's Barn, Teffont, Salisbury, Wiltshire SP3 5QP

CHOOSE A PHOTOGRAPH FROM THIS BOOK

Voucher *for FREE and Reduced Price Frith Prints*

Please do not photocopy this voucher. Only the original is valid, so please fill it in, cut it out and return it to us with your order.

Picture ref no	Page no	Qty	Mounted @ £7.49	Framed + £14.95	Total Cost £
		1	Free of charge*	£	£
			£7.49	£	£
			£7.49	£	£
			£7.49	£	£
			£7.49	£	£
			£7.49	£	£

Please allow 28 days for delivery. Offer available to one UK address only

* Post & handling	£3.50
Total Order Cost	£

Title of this book . . . .

I enclose a cheque/postal order for £ . . . . made payable to 'The Francis Frith Collection'

OR please debit my Mastercard / Visa / Maestro card, details below

Card Number

Issue No (Maestro only)   Valid from (Maestro)

Expires   Signature

Name Mr/Mrs/Ms . . . .

Address . . . .

. . . .

. . . .

. . . . Postcode . . . .

Daytime Tel No . . . .

Email . . . .

ISBN 1-84589-149-X   Valid to 31/12/09

Can you help us with information about any of the Frith photographs in this book?

We are gradually compiling an historical record for each of the photographs in the Frith archive. It is always fascinating to find out the names of the people shown in the pictures, as well as insights into the shops, buildings and other features depicted.

If you recognize anyone in the photographs in this book, or if you have information not already included in the author's caption, do let us know. We would love to hear from you, and will try to publish it in future books or articles.

Our production team

Frith books are produced by a small dedicated team at offices in the converted Grade II listed 18th-century barn at Teffont near Salisbury, illustrated above. Most have worked with The Francis Frith Collection for many years. All have in common one quality: they have a passion for The Francis Frith Collection. The team is constantly expanding, but currently includes:

Andrew Alsop, Paul Baron, Jason Buck, John Buck, Jenny Coles, Heather Crisp, David Davies, Natalie Davis, Louis du Mont, Isobel Hall, Chris Hardwick, Neil Harvey, Julian Hight, Peter Horne, James Kinnear, Karen Kinnear, Tina Leary, Stuart Login, Sue Molloy, Sarah Roberts, Kate Rotondetto, Eliza Sackett, Terence Sackett, Sandra Sampson, Adrian Sanders, Sandra Sanger, Julia Skinner, Lewis Taylor, Will Tunnicliffe, David Turner and Ricky Williams.